HEALING YOUR INNER CHILD

RECOVERING FROM CHILDHOOD TRAUMA AND RESTORING SELF-LOVE

JD Landor

Copyright © 2020 JD Landor

All rights reserved.

ISBN:

CONTENTS

INTRODUCTION 1
WRAPPING YOUR HEAD AND ARMS AROUND IT 3
   1. Who is your inner child? 3
   2. What are the qualities of your inner child? 4
   3. What is your inner child capable of? 5
   4. Why should your inner child be healed? 6
   5. How do you heal your inner child? 6
      a.   Understand the specific predicament that your inner child is going through 7
      b.   Speak and/or write to your inner child to calm them down 7
      c.   Talk cordially to your inner child 8
      d.   Seek professional or non-professional help 8

IN AND AROUND FORGIVENESS 11
   6. What is the essence of looking at forgiveness? 11
   7. Who should you forgive for hurting your inner child? 12
   8. What happens when you forgive your offenders? 14
   9. How do you forgive your offenders? 15

SHIFTING THE FOCUS: POSITIVE CHILDHOOD EXPERIENCES 19
   10. Why should you think about your positive

childhood experiences? 20

11. What were some good things about your childhood? 22

12. How can you connect with your positive childhood experiences? 23

13. How can your inner child benefit from the good in your toddler life? 25

CHANGE OF SCENE..27

CONCLUSION 35

INTRODUCTION

This is for you – you whose inner child is banging against the walls that surround it. From the inside, your inner child has made it clear that they need attention, and they need it fast. This – this is for you.

Organized into four parts, this book explores one of the most sensitive subjects in recent times – mental health.

I hope that you find the material to nurse the injury and alleviate the pain.

I pray that you overcome your predicament.

I wish that you get healing.

Go for it.

PART I: WRAPPING YOUR HEAD AND ARMS AROUND IT

1. Who is your inner child?

Your inner child is a mini-version of you who exists in a space that psychologists call the unconscious. Our mental focus may not be on the unconscious but more often than not, we tend to operate from its point. This is an argument that Sigmund Freud, the great psychoanalyst would have advanced effortlessly.

To simplify, your inner child is the person you were when you were a child. This person keeps coming and going as you live your adulthood. Something unique about childhood is that it never dies just because you advance in age. It continues to live as a mini-person (or a sub-personality) that is popularly known as the inner child.

Have you ever heard someone being referred to as a big baby? If you have, then the person (who was an adult) was exhibiting childlike mannerisms. You can say that at that time, their inner child jumped out of their unconscious and got activated.

2. What are the qualities of your inner child?

This question is meant to inform you about what your inner child is made of, which is quite simple. The entirety of your childhood experiences forms your inner child. This should communicate to you how impactful childhood experiences are to the life of an adult. Your childhood experiences can are either be positive or negative ones.

It is important to mention that of interest in this book are the negative experiences, those that bring about childhood injuries. Speaking of negative experiences, these can be sorted into abuse (physical, verbal and/or sexual) and neglect (lack of attention and resources such as food, shelter etcetera). In many cases, these experiences have a traumatic effect 💔 that penetrates a person's adult life.

3. What is your inner child capable of?

As mentioned in the answer to the previous question, childhood experiences have a great impact on your adult life. Negative experiences form a great part of how we live our adulthood. So, the inner child exhibits themselves in different ways as shown in the examples:

Q. An unattended person may exhibit clingy behaviour in their adulthood.
Q. A person who was verbally abused may blow an insult out of proportion.
Q. A person who did not get enough food may hold their plate to themselves.

Many people will term these reactions as immature – the adjective used for children. Yet, they are merely expressions of the inner child. This shows you how the inner child is capable of influencing adult life.

4. Why should your inner child be healed?

This is the most important question, yet it is the one that is least asked. Many people who seek for inner child healing want to know how to go about it and not why it is necessary. In this part, you will look at the reasons why it is important. Of the many, three reasons why you should seek inner healing is that it will help you:

Q Establish control over your emotions as an adult,
Q Focus on working on and achieving your goals and;
Q Live a life that is free from strife.

The task here is to know the reason why you want healing. On your healing process, your reason(s) will become your motivation.

5. How do you heal your inner child?

a. Understand the specific predicament that your inner child is going through

With this solution, you are supposed to take a trip back to when you were a child. Look at all the people in your upbringing and what they took you through. Be specific about the retrospection and isolate the negative experiences. Write all of them in a paper. This may be painful but it is necessary.

Of the experiences that you have isolated, sort them out in terms of the effect they had on you. The one that had the greatest (traumatic) effect should come first. With this exercise, you have opened your mind into understanding the predicaments of your inner child.

b. Speak and/or write to your inner child to calm them down

Engaging in the retrospection (in the previous how) should have put you in touch with your inner child in an overwhelming way. You now understand why it is hurting and the kind of injuries that it is nursing. What you now need to do it to communicate with it.

Establishing communication with your inner child is actually connecting with your feelings. So, you need to do it with pacification – be as calm as the waters of the Pacific. This will prevent you from hurting yourself. Your letter or speech should acknowledge the fact that you understand what the child is going through. Also, it should be an assurance that things will be better.

c.   Talk cordially to your inner child

This is supposed to beef up what you have started in the previous how. Look at the following lines:

Dear inner child, I need peace of mind,

To you, I will be kind, and your happiness, I will find.

The emotional energy in and around the above lines is that you need to be fair. Although it is affecting your adulthood, your inner child is guilty of nothing. It needs warmth and deserves to hear cordialities.

On rationality, you need to talk to your inner child about forgiving the people who made it go through awful experiences. You should pardon the people who left painful, indelible marks when you were new to the world.

d. Seek professional or non-professional help

In the previous responses (a, b and c), you were engaging in self-therapy. You were making steps in understanding and communicating with your inner child. Now, you are ready to walk up to a listener and speak for and about your inner child.

On professional help, you can seek the services of a psychotherapist or a counselling psychologist. Look up the nearest psychological clinic around you and book an appointment. They have the credentials and will guide you appropriately.

On non-professional help, you can make a date with a friend or a relation of yours. This person should not judge you for who you are but should give you undivided attention. Whichever you choose, remember to present the results of your self-therapy to them.

PART II: IN AND AROUND FORGIVENESS

6. What is the essence of looking at forgiveness?

Whenever people discuss human struggles, there is a big chance that the issue of forgiving will come up. From time to time, therapists and psychologists have seen that forgiveness, or the action of it has a significant effect on our struggles. In this book, the focus is on the troubles of the inner child. This question is supposed to speak to you about why you should think about forgiveness.

In this book, these words will summarize

forgiveness: unburdening and deleting. Unburdening is laying off a load while deleting is letting the load slip away from your long-term memory. The load, in this case, is the helplessness of your inner child. Your inner child is weak and easily gets offended. Its nature weighs it down and puts it in a vulnerable position, which means that it affects you.

The be-all and end-all of looking at forgiveness is this – absolute contentment. Forgiveness unburdens and deletes a load that the inner child carries. The inner child then becomes freer, happier and more exuberant. Although hurt, it gains particular confidence. This confidence has a ripple effect on the adult. Adulthood becomes more of a challenge to be taken up than a burden to be borne. At the heart of forgiveness lies absolute contentment.

7. Who should you forgive for hurting your inner child?

Having established the need for forgiveness in your pursuit of healing, it is imperative that you now identify the persons of interest. These persons of interest are those who inflicted/inflict pain to your inner child. Your inner child is affected by real persons, not forces. With this question, you are going to take your mind back to your childhood and bring it forward to your adulthood.

The persons of interest who will now be called offenders are in two groups:

Q. The first group is the people who brought you up. When you came into the world and were fortunate enough, you had adults whose responsibility was to bring you up. It could have been your parents, guardians or siblings. These people who helped you socialize with the world could also have abused or neglected you.

Q. The other group is of those who are part of your adulthood. Yes – some of the people you know now may have injured or are injuring your inner child. Have you ever emotionally expressed yourself and been told that you are being immature? If yes – did you feel hurt? If the answer is yes too, it means that your inner child was affected.

Adulthood is a societal construction that, in a way, suppresses emotional expression and advocates for reason and sense. On the flip side, childhood is in the shape of emotions. Now, you know who to place in whatever group, don't you?

Note: This is not supposed to trigger any reactions towards the people in your life. It is just empowerment through knowledge, alright?

8. What happens when you forgive your offenders?

At this point, you know who the offender(s) are. You know who is guilty of making your inner child whimper, sob and break into a loud and teary cry. I would like to remind you that you are not supposed to react in any way towards them. You need to establish total control over your emotions. With that note regurgitated, the question in hand will now be addressed.

In the question about the essence of forgiveness, a

phrase stood out: absolute contentment. The phrase succinctly responds to this question. Absolute contentment is a prerequisite for happiness or the feeling of it. When we forgive, we take steps in the journey of satisfaction. Your inner child's load affects you. In turn, you become unhappy. People don't understand where you are coming from and who you are. So, they don't treat you like you as supposed to be treated. Imagine if we all knew and understood that people are struggling with injuries such as a vulnerable inner child. Wouldn't we be treating people differently, especially when they choose to express their emotions in their raw form? Wouldn't we have treated that tantrum that that friend threw in a more informed, calm and considerate way? Wouldn't the world be happier?

Since it will be hard to get everyone to understand our struggle, we need to forgive them to become happier. This happiness, as said here comes about because of absolute contentment.

9. How do you forgive your offenders?

Forgiveness is easy to talk about but difficult to embrace. However, you should overlook the element of difficulty and pursue it. Remember that forgiveness, or seeking it is supposed to unlock happiness through absolute contentment. This question is arguably the most crucial one in this part and the response will be tailored with the gravitas it deserves.

As they say, forgiveness should be deliberate and uncompelled. Deliberate means that you should mean to forgive your offender. You have to accept in your heart and mind that you want to do it. On the other hand, uncompelled means that it should be done willingly and not when you're under pressure.

At this moment, you know your offenders. You may have been neglected by your parent or abused by a relative. Also, your genuine emotions may have been called out as childish by a colleague, a friend or an acquaintance. These people have made the list. What you now need to do is to forgive them. It may be achieved if the following steps are made:

Q. Accept that things have already happened. The damage cannot be undone and neither the experiences erased. It will allow you to live with the injuries.

Q. Declare that you want to work on unburdening yourself off the weight that your offenders make you carry. You can write the declaration on a piece of paper and read it from time to time. Also, you can record a video of yourself making that declaration. Play it at least once a day, a week or something there in between.

Q. Tell your inner child not to bear any resentment towards its offenders. Here, you will need to engage in lots of self-talk. You should tell your inner child something like this, 'Forgive them precious, they didn't know what they did to you.'

Q. Speak to any of your offenders in a move to forgive them, if you can. This step applies if your childhood was affected immensely, say, by repeated sexual, physical or verbal abuse or something of the same weight. Sit them down and tell them that you are seeking healing for your inner child. Don't ask them why they did what they did – inform them calmly and tactfully that they did it. Importantly, make them know that you have nothing against them and you are extending an olive branch.

PART III: SHIFTING THE FOCUS: POSITIVE CHILDHOOD EXPERIENCES

Whenever the phrase inner child is mentioned, a negative connotation is, by default, assigned to it. The inner child is always bruised, weak, helpless and in great turmoil. In fact, the subtitle of this book, Healing Your Inner Child makes it clear that the inner child is broken down, suffering and diseased. The inner child or its character is the total of her experiences, both the negative and the positive ones. So, it is logical to say that this perspective that is shared among many people, experts and non-experts, is blatantly biased.

This part intends to guide you into looking at your

positive childhood experiences. This is a total shift from the popular, negative focal point. The questions will guide you into looking at the pleasant events and the wholesome happenings in your childhood. These are what will be referred to as positive childhood experiences. Enjoy the positivity and take in the goodness.

10. Why should you think about your positive childhood experiences?

It has already been made clear that this part is nothing but a bed of roses. Taking on this velvet pursuit is supposed to bring your inner child to a different, better place. Pursuing that positivity, you need to reminiscence about your childhood. Before this pursuit is made, however, you should know why you are even doing it. What is the why and wherefore for doing this? Is it necessary to even think about positivity when all you have is a darkened form of the inner child?

A research was done by paediatric experts about

the effect of positive childhood experiences on the mental health of adults. The finding was that those who have warmer childhoods are less likely to experience mental illnesses than those whose childhoods were troubled. There will be an attempt to link this scientific finding with the subject of this part.

Was your childhood entirely dark? If your answer to this question is yes, that is unfortunate and to a great extent, unreasonable. It would be hard to believe there was no moment of bliss in your childhood, isn't it? In this world, there is abject poverty but arguably, there is no such thing as extreme sadness.

With this in mind, we can create a link between science and the subject herein. If positive childhood experiences reflect well in our adult lives, would thinking and talking about them improve the situation of our inner child? It would be like telling this to the inner child, 'Hey, precious, life had its hitches but it still had its moments of bliss. It is true that you, or let's say we were neglected, abuse or injured in a way, but, surely, there is something worth celebrating.' Therefore, the reason why you need to think about the positives of your childhood is that they have the potential to improve your present situation. Your current situation can receive the touch of milk and honey it needs if you focus on the good things about your childhood.

11. What were some good things about your childhood?

Since you now know the importance of the blissful bits of your childhood, you are motivated and ready to reminisce about those good times. With this motivation, you can now walk back to the past, filter out the darkness and give complete attention to the light.

This should be an exercise that you do on your own. Make the following simple, relaxing and introspective steps:

Q. Sit or lie down in a space where you are alone. This could be a room, an amusement part or an abandoned building. Don't forget about your safety in this escapade.

Q. Close your eyes and organise your imagination. You are the only person who can take yourself where you need to be.

Q. Collect the good moments and make sure your smile whenever one comes up. Whenever the dark moments flash, try to repress them. Take your time.

Q. Quit the imagination and take a writing pad. Then, write this section's question. With your imaginative experience, list your answers.

At this point, you have made a lot of success organizing the positives from your childhood. How does it feel? It must be a good if not an exhilarating feeling. Now, you are in a better place.

12. How can you connect with your positive childhood experiences?

At this point, you should be experiencing a feel-good feeling. You have fished out a list of treasures from a pile of manure. Now, you will need to move to a position where you are connected with the treasures you listed. Your list of good things may not be a long one, but this is going to change.

To build a connection with your positive childhood experiences and add to your treasure list, you need to bring in some human help. You need to have sit-downs with the people who brought you up or the ones who you were around growing up. These people may have even inflicted pain on you, but the sit-downs will take a different trajectory.

When you plan to meet up with your connectors, you need to ready yourself. What you want from them are the positives. So, the questions you can ask them is all or any of these:

Q. When I was a child, what good things did I do or say?

Q. In my childhood, was there any moment you felt like I was the sweetest thing ever?

Believe it or not – you will feel your childhood

being sweetened. Your connectors will take you back to your life – your former, toddler life.

13. How can your inner child benefit from the good in your toddler life?

Getting to this point means that you have made great steps in the journey of positivity. With all the steps and all the findings, you need to know how your inner child can benefit. When you started this healing pursuit, you were on the receiving end of a troubled childhood. Now, you know that your inner child is made of more.

You will need to engage in a couple of self-therapy sessions with your inner child. Your greatest tool during this self-therapy sessions is self-talk. Tell your inner child that life is greener on the other side. Speak to it about all the positive things that you have learned about in the previous questions. In turn, your inner child will disengage from its foetal position. Slowly, it will grow out of the intimidation and fright that had been weighing it down. Although broken, the vision of healing that had been blurred will become crystal clear.

This self-therapy sessions work in the same way as self-motivation does. Motivational speakers guide their audience to speak forward-looking, productive and efficacious things to themselves. The positives that you outline for your inner child will keep it and you confident that things will get better.

"Hey, precious, how are you? I know that you're feeling terrible at this moment. But, I'd like to tell you something. You used to make your friends smile by sharing your lunch with them. It made you feel nice when they told you how much of a blessing you were to them. You may not feel as fair and lovely now as you did then but trust me when I say that things will get better".

PART IV: LIFE IS BEAUTIFUL. CHANGE OF SCENE

Life is beautiful and it should be lived to the fullest. Being alive is more than just taking in air into our lungs and breathing it out. Our existence is meaningful. We matter regardless of our present situation or past experiences. Our experiences, whether good or bad, should serve and not victimize us but that is not always the case. We crumble and get broken by people. Also, situations from our past enslave us and take away our happiness. What we experience growing up plays a big role in shaping who we become as adults.

These experiences shape our thought process, decision-making patterns, our attitudes about life and how we see ourselves among other aspects. Negative experiences in our childhood haunt us later in our adult life. Most of the time, we are unaware of the missing link to our present undesirable state because it is buried deep in our unconscious mind. It becomes an unseen, poisoned source that pollutes our current stream which is our conscious mind. This is sabotage of the self that happens from within.

One can get trapped in this bubble that robs them of the peace in their lives. This happens as a result of unresolved childhood traumas. Childhood traumas are events or experiences that cause extreme emotional pain and distress resulting in lasting mental and physical effects. Having a wounded inner child makes an adult live out their childhood fears through their grown-up eyes. Those negative and unresolved memories are the reason for the manifestation of a broken inner child in an adult.

The manifestations of a traumatizing past present themselves in defective behavioural, mental, and emotional patterns. These include anger, trust and attachment issues, passive-aggressive behaviour and a defective sense of self. Others are overindulging habits, perpetual victimization, poor memory and an altered state of consciousness.

However, these facts should not cause despair to anyone struggling with their inner child. There is hope and a way out. It is possible to get help and renew your life through therapy. The decision has to come from you. You have to want to change first before achieving it. Your present life does not have to be chaotic for you to make a move. Also, you don't have to be deeply struggling with aspects of yourself to have a turnaround. It should start with a single emotion. It should come from your heart. If you feel that something is missing in your life and you cannot point it out, go back in time and reconnect with your inner child. It is time to have a consultation with them, find out any problems, solve them and move on.

To connect with your inner child will start your healing and recovery process. You can start by reflecting on your childhood memories and create a timeline. Try not to skip the moments when you experienced trauma. It helps to use past videos if you have any. Also, photos or visiting places can help you recall.

Write down these events with every emotion you experienced then and now. It is okay to feel sad and cry because it means that you have finally gained the courage to face your worst fears and address your pains. It means that it is no longer a hidden secret kept in the dark corner of your mind anymore. This is a sign that you are freeing your mind. Also, you are gaining the power to address all the hurt you have gone through.

Write a letter to your inner child. When doing this, remember to use kind words and speak positively. Be like a guardian angel to your little self, encouraging them to be strong and assuring them of protection and love. Tell them that they are beautiful and very important. Tell them that it is okay for them to be scared because they are merely children and it is not their fault that bad things happened to them. Mention the things you would have loved to hear during your childhood that would have made a difference. Exhaust everything.

Write a second letter from your inner child to yourself as the guardian angel. Write about the things you have witnessed that were not right. The things and people that made you afraid. Speak about the times you were happy and sad during those memories. Express yourself the same way you would have in your childhood. That is, if you had the chance to speak up freely or if you had someone to talk to. You can keep writing between these two personas until you feel comfortable to stop. It should feel like you as a child but with a confidant to guide through tough times. There is power in speaking up. You are going to break down many walls that had been built in your mind for years.

The next step is to find someone you can trust and share your story and pain with. It can be a friend or a therapist. Don't hold back because of fear or shame. Remember that the more you talk about it the lesser it burdens you. This will help you gain the confidence to work on bettering yourself. At this point, you will realize that it is time for you to start forgiving.

Why forgive? We forgive so that we can be free. An unforgiving heart makes us bitter and angry. You create a sad grave for yourself when you hold on to the hurt that happened to you. To be able to forgive, accept that what happened to you as an indirect gift for you to take a new, different path in life. Counter those hurtful thoughts with feelings of gratitude. Be strong for you to survive.

Understand that you might not get justice or closure for what happened to you. That sounds unfair but is the way the world is. You might not get an apology from the person who hurt you and they may never feel any kind of remorse for their actions towards you. Forgive them anyway. Make simple steps to help you close that chapter of your life completely. Cut any type of links you had with this person. Cut all communication. It is okay to move away to a different town if you can. Shut them out for your own sake. The way to do this is to put yourself first and focus on your goals.

A positive thing to do during this period is to start engaging in activities that support your journey. Join a support group and make friends who can help you walk your journey. Start doing yoga to help you find your core, taking the time to connect with your inner child in the process. It is also important to start listening to love and supportive affirmations.

Start meditating and visualizing as well. Meditation is a great way to work on your inner self. Also, treat yourself in a sterling way. Start exercising. Take yourself out and buy yourself a gift that will make you feel good. You can get a new haircut or a wardrobe change. You can paint your room or house a different colour. Get enough sleep and remember to balance your work with your personal life.

Your inner child is that part of you that reacts and feels like a child. Let us not allow what happened to us in the past define us for the rest of our lives. We can rise above those experiences and heal from within.

CONCLUSION

Healing Your Inner Child is an evocative book whose work is one – to guide you to the healing of your inner child. If you have faithfully come this far, you should be in a different place emotionally and mentally. You should be empowered, motivated and confident that your inner child will be healed.

It is strongly recommended that you seek the services of a professional therapist or psychologist. This book will shape how you express your situation to them.

This book informs you and gets you acquainted with almost everything you need to know about your inner child. With a read, you are in a better place and in charge of your situation.

Be safe.

Manufactured by Amazon.ca
Bolton, ON